Road to Healing

Rosemary Trujillo

Copyright © 2019 Rosemary Trujillo.

All rights reserved. No part of this book may be used or reproduced by any means, graphic, electronic, or mechanical, including photocopying, recording, taping or by any information storage retrieval system without the written permission of the author except in the case of brief quotations embodied in critical articles and reviews.

This book is a work of non-fiction. Unless otherwise noted, the author and the publisher make no explicit guarantees as to the accuracy of the information contained in this book and in some cases, names of people and places have been altered to protect their privacy.

Archway Publishing books may be ordered
through booksellers or by contacting:

Archway Publishing
1663 Liberty Drive
Bloomington, IN 47403
www.archwaypublishing.com
1 (888) 242-5904

Because of the dynamic nature of the Internet, any web addresses or links contained in this book may have changed since publication and may no longer be valid. The views expressed in this work are solely those of the author and do not necessarily reflect the views of the publisher, and the publisher hereby disclaims any responsibility for them.

Any people depicted in stock imagery provided by Getty Images are models, and such images are being used for illustrative purposes only. Certain stock imagery © Getty Images.

ISBN: 978-1-4808-8374-1 (sc)
ISBN: 978-1-4808-8375-8 (e)

Library of Congress Control Number: 2019917291

Print information available on the last page.

Archway Publishing rev. date: 11/01/2019

Dedicated to Julie Anné, founder of A New Beginning, and Caitie Canacakos, founder of Empowered Lifestyle

The light is shining as a sign from above.
The waves are soothing and full of love.
The sand is cold between our toes.
The heart is filled with a smile that glows.
This is the day you begin to heal,
To follow your dreams—and this time for real.

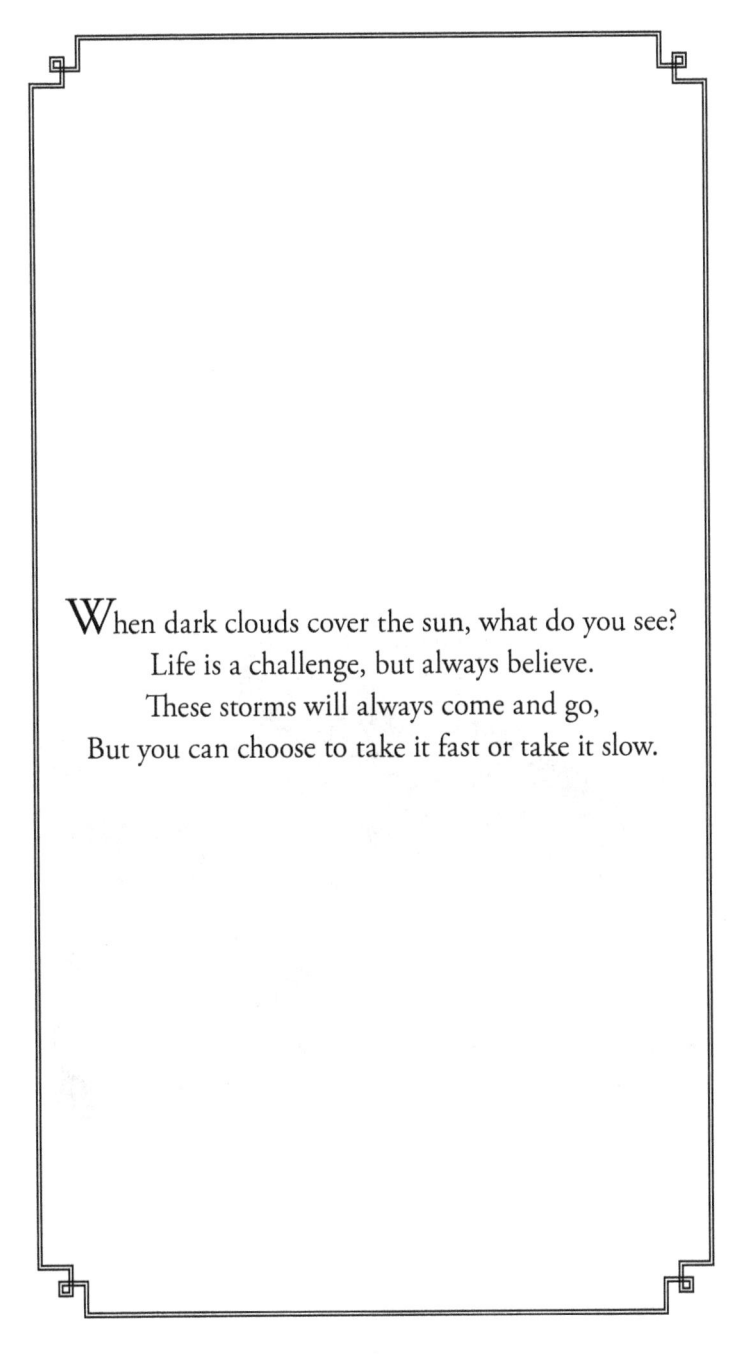

When dark clouds cover the sun, what do you see?
Life is a challenge, but always believe.
These storms will always come and go,
But you can choose to take it fast or take it slow.

Reading is a way to help your mind and soul.
It takes you to another world,
where life is not so dull—
Places you have seen a thousand
times or never been before.
Adventures you don't forget, no
matter how much you explore.

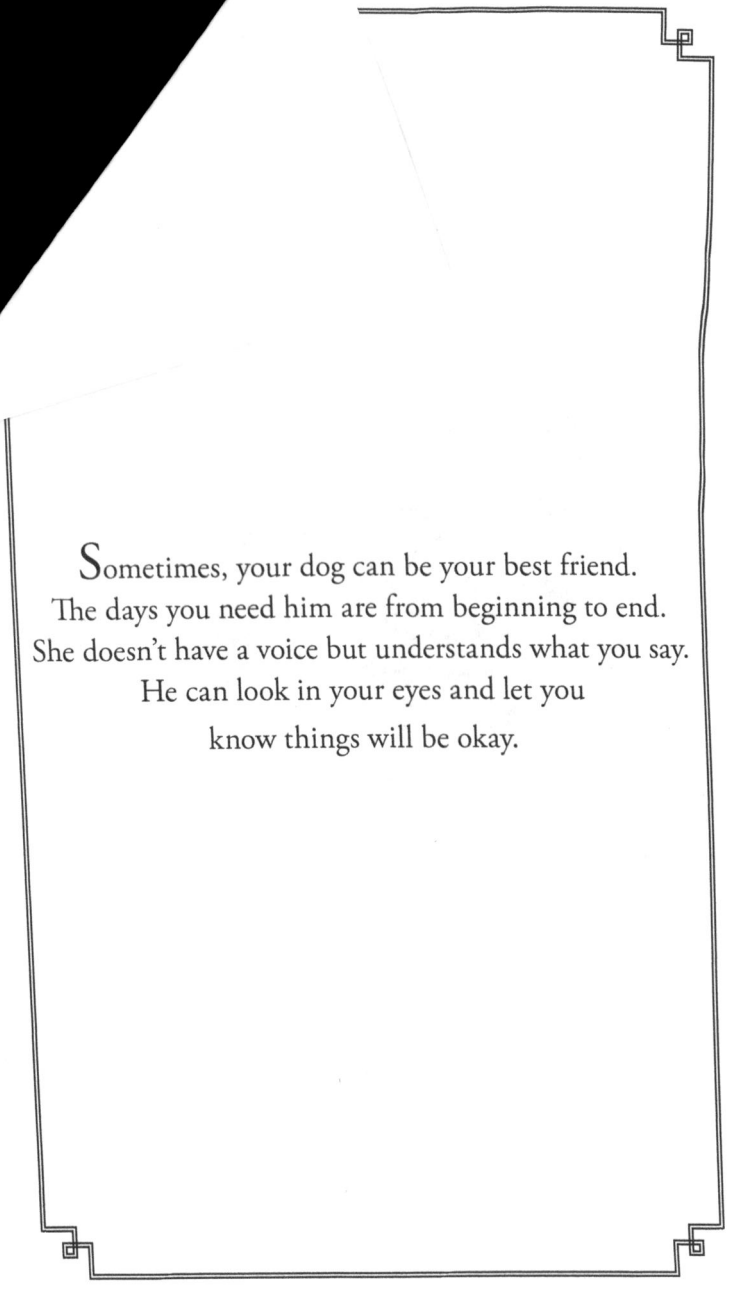

Sometimes, your dog can be your best friend.
The days you need him are from beginning to end.
She doesn't have a voice but understands what you say.
He can look in your eyes and let you
know things will be okay.

Sometimes, we struggle and doubt
ourselves when climbing to the top.

We let fear take over our minds and
don't know when to stop.

We take a break so we have the strength
to complete what we have begun.

We know with all our confidence,
this challenge can be done.

Sisters are our best friends that last forever.

We laugh, we cry, and we always stick together.

No matter if we're close or far apart,

We are always connected heart to heart.

This is where my life began, a small
mining town by Miami.

The place I loved most was the store
filled with all the candy.

The water that rapidly flowed down
my childhood street,

The nights my mom called out, "It's
time to come in and eat,"

The neighbors and friends that I played with every day,

The walk home from the swimming pool
each summer starting in May.

We climbed the mountains till we
could climb no more—

Memories I cherish as I close that door.

A father and son will stand side by side;

The love they share is something you can't hide.

They have a special bond and trust to
keep them from drifting apart,

Something they will cherish forever as one
keeps the other close to his heart.

Our lives are reflections of what
decisions we choose to make.
We deal with what we can until we break.
We have to be brave and always try and try again.
What comes next is to move forward
from where we have been.

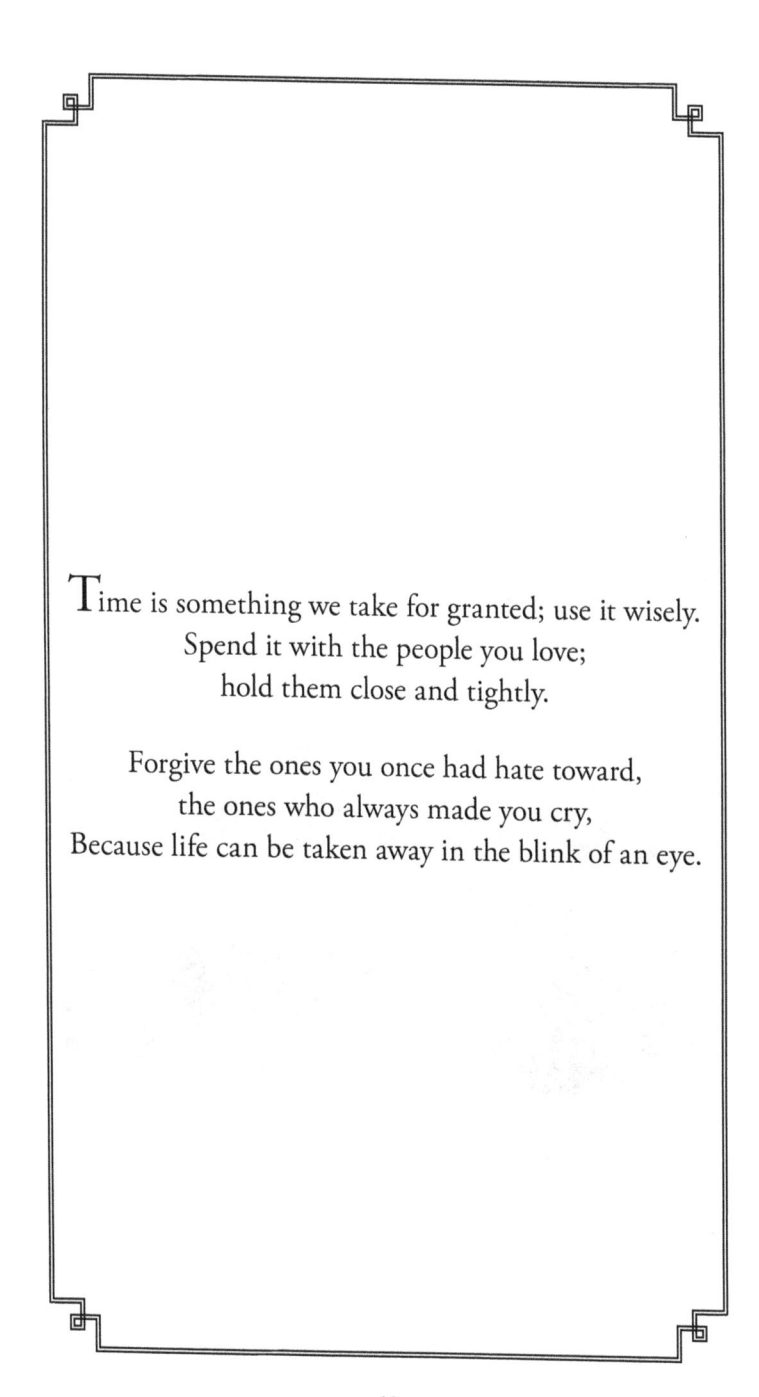

Time is something we take for granted; use it wisely.
Spend it with the people you love;
hold them close and tightly.

Forgive the ones you once had hate toward,
the ones who always made you cry,
Because life can be taken away in the blink of an eye.

A New Beginning is a place we gain
power that was once taken away.

It gives us hope and a chance to live a
life without the fear of each day.

We learn that we can heal from our
shame and love ourselves within.

It leads us to the place where we slowly trust again.

It is a woman of great words and
wisdom in helping us to fight.

The day we walk out the door is when
we know it's going to be all right.

Yoga is the thing you do to silence your mind.

You learn how to breathe slowly and put
all your bad thoughts behind.

Yoga helps you find peace and
happiness to forget your fears.

The energy it brings are words that soothe
our souls and help the tears.

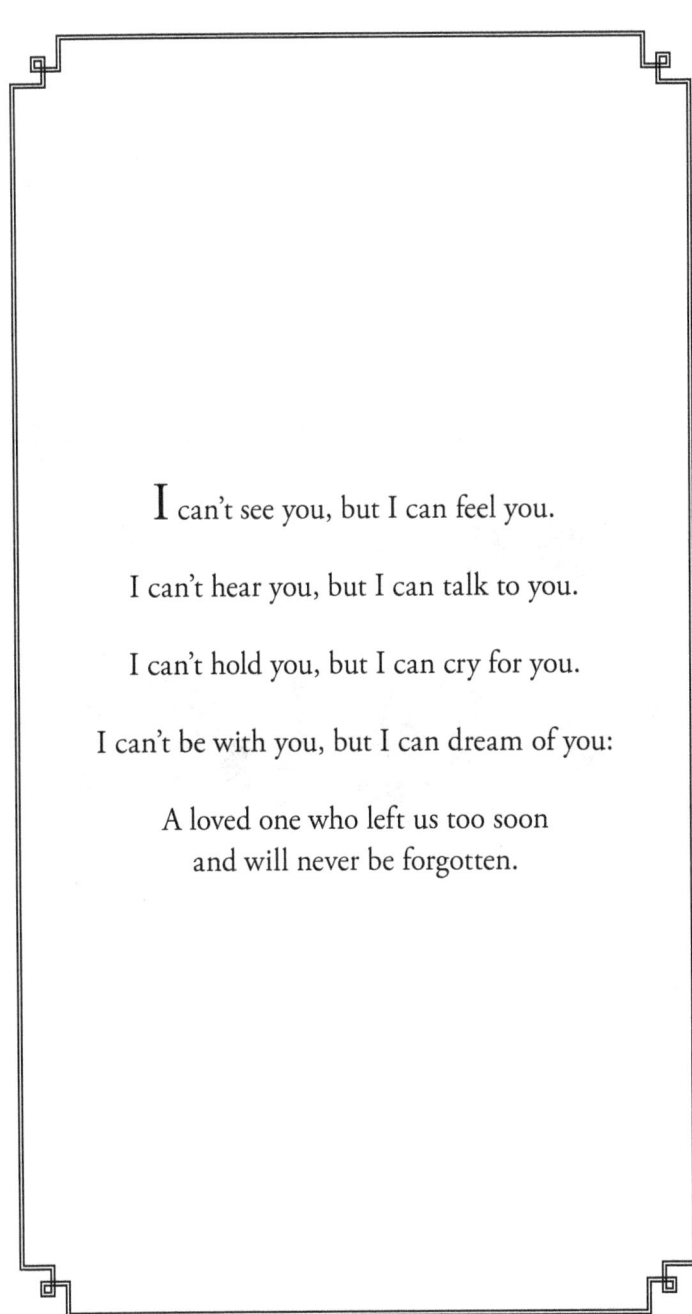

I can't see you, but I can feel you.

I can't hear you, but I can talk to you.

I can't hold you, but I can cry for you.

I can't be with you, but I can dream of you:

> A loved one who left us too soon
> and will never be forgotten.

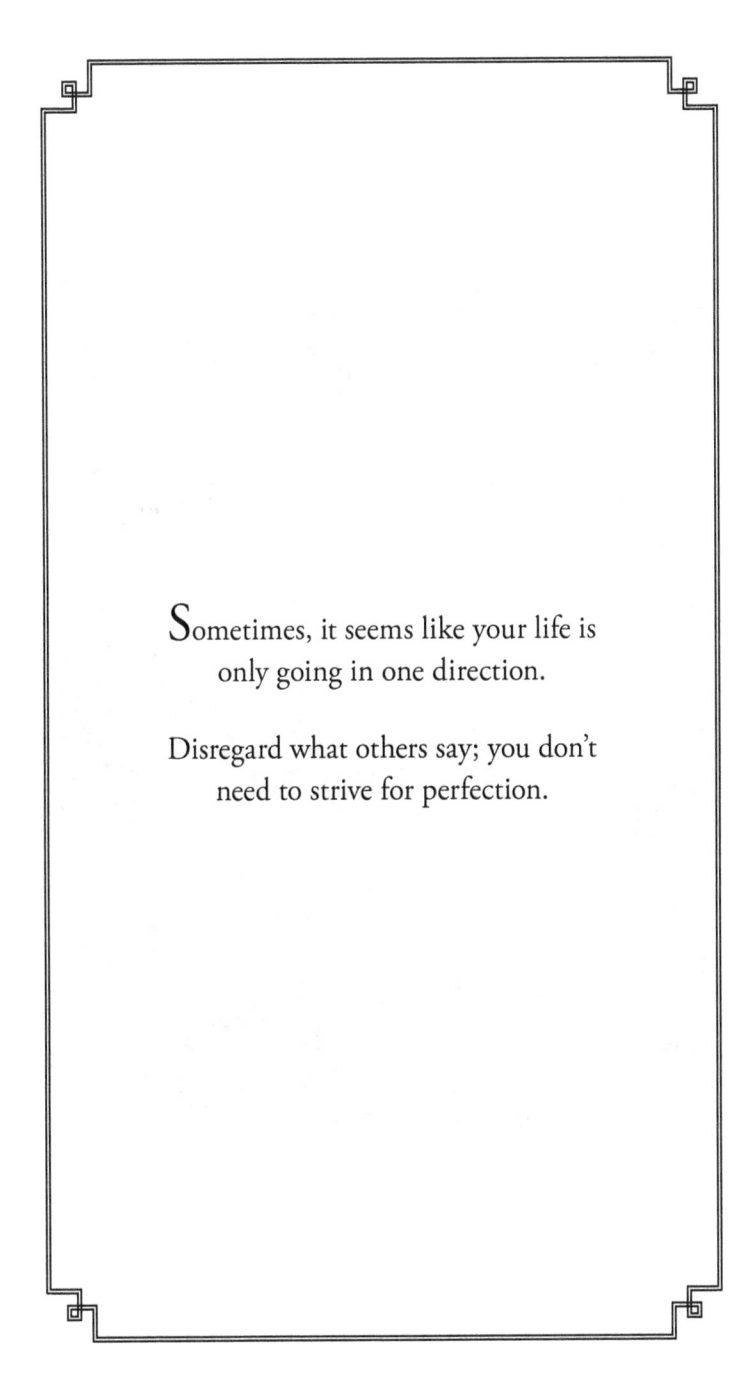

Sometimes, it seems like your life is only going in one direction.

Disregard what others say; you don't need to strive for perfection.

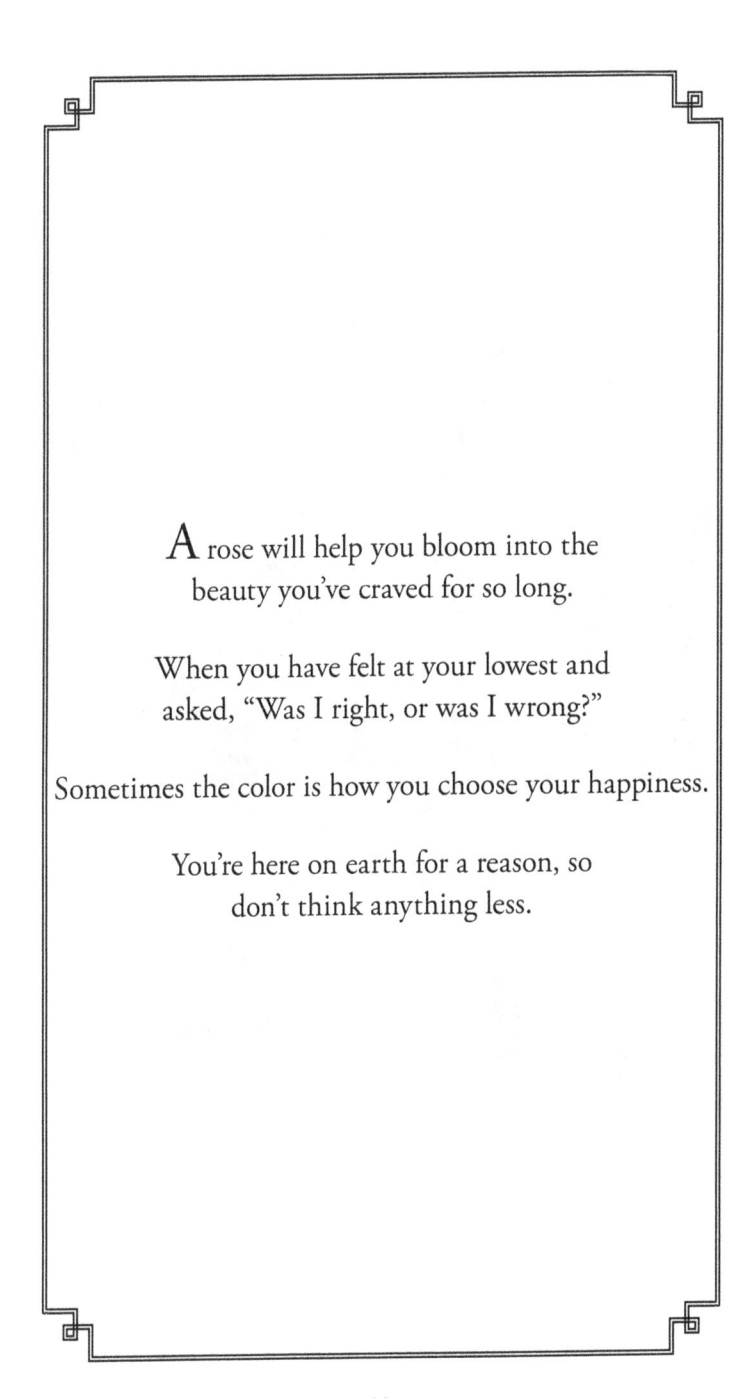

A rose will help you bloom into the
beauty you've craved for so long.

When you have felt at your lowest and
asked, "Was I right, or was I wrong?"

Sometimes the color is how you choose your happiness.

You're here on earth for a reason, so
don't think anything less.

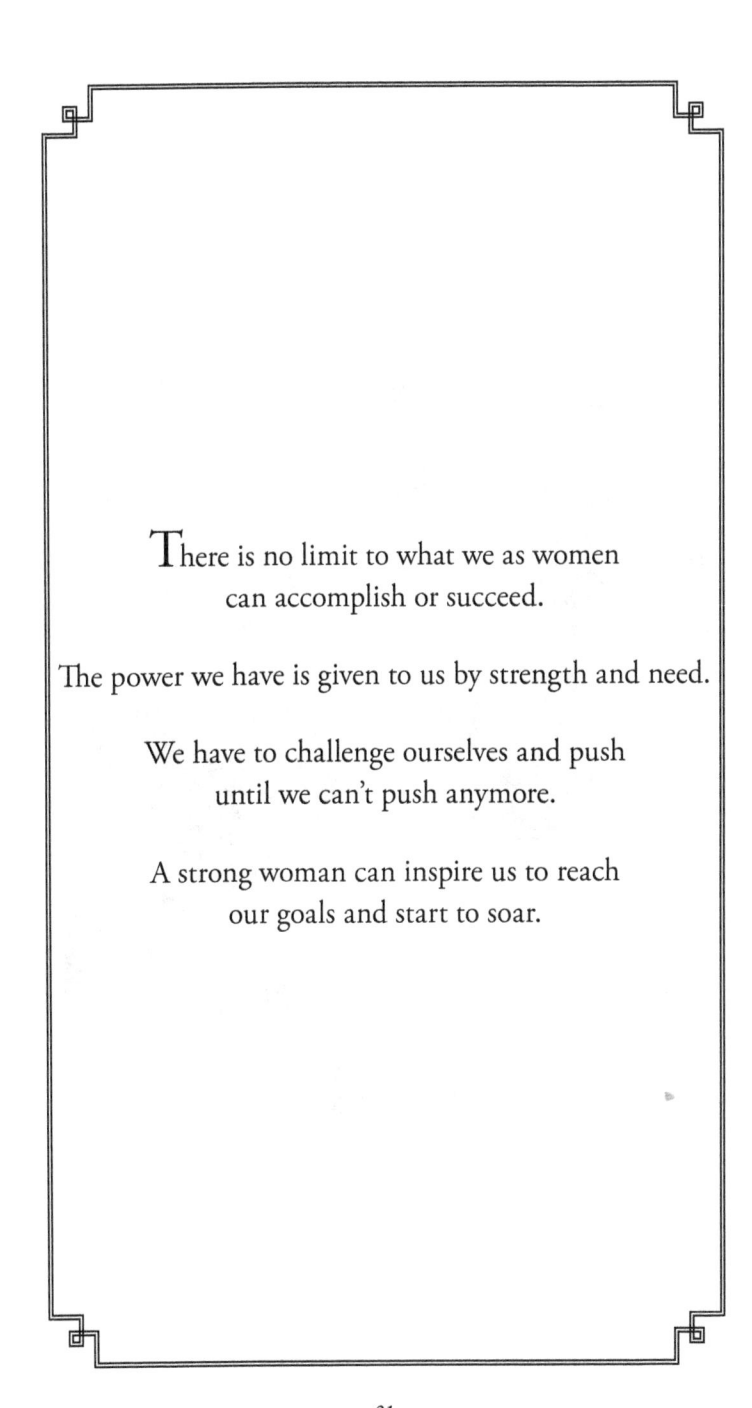

There is no limit to what we as women
can accomplish or succeed.

The power we have is given to us by strength and need.

We have to challenge ourselves and push
until we can't push anymore.

A strong woman can inspire us to reach
our goals and start to soar.

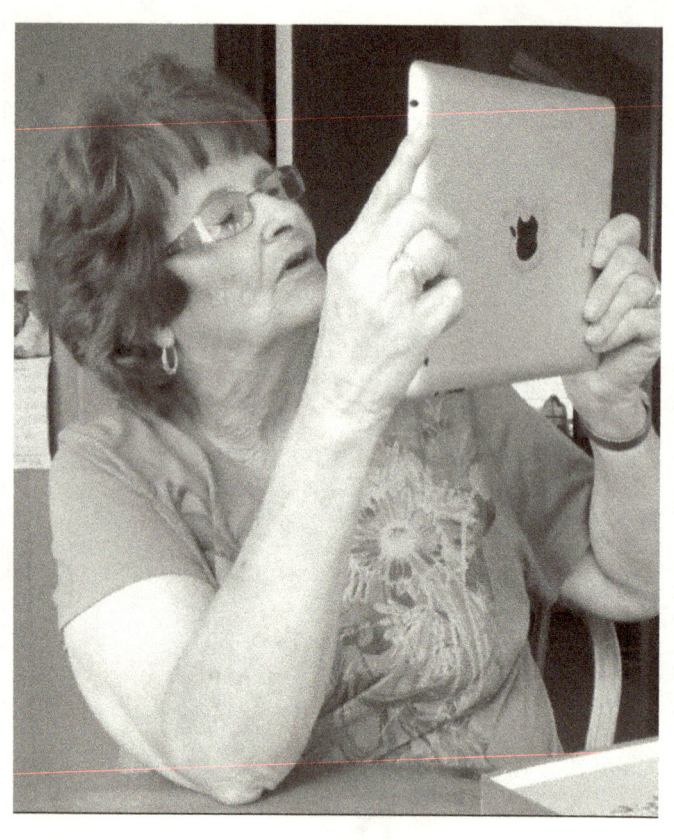

How do you see yourself as you look into a mirror?

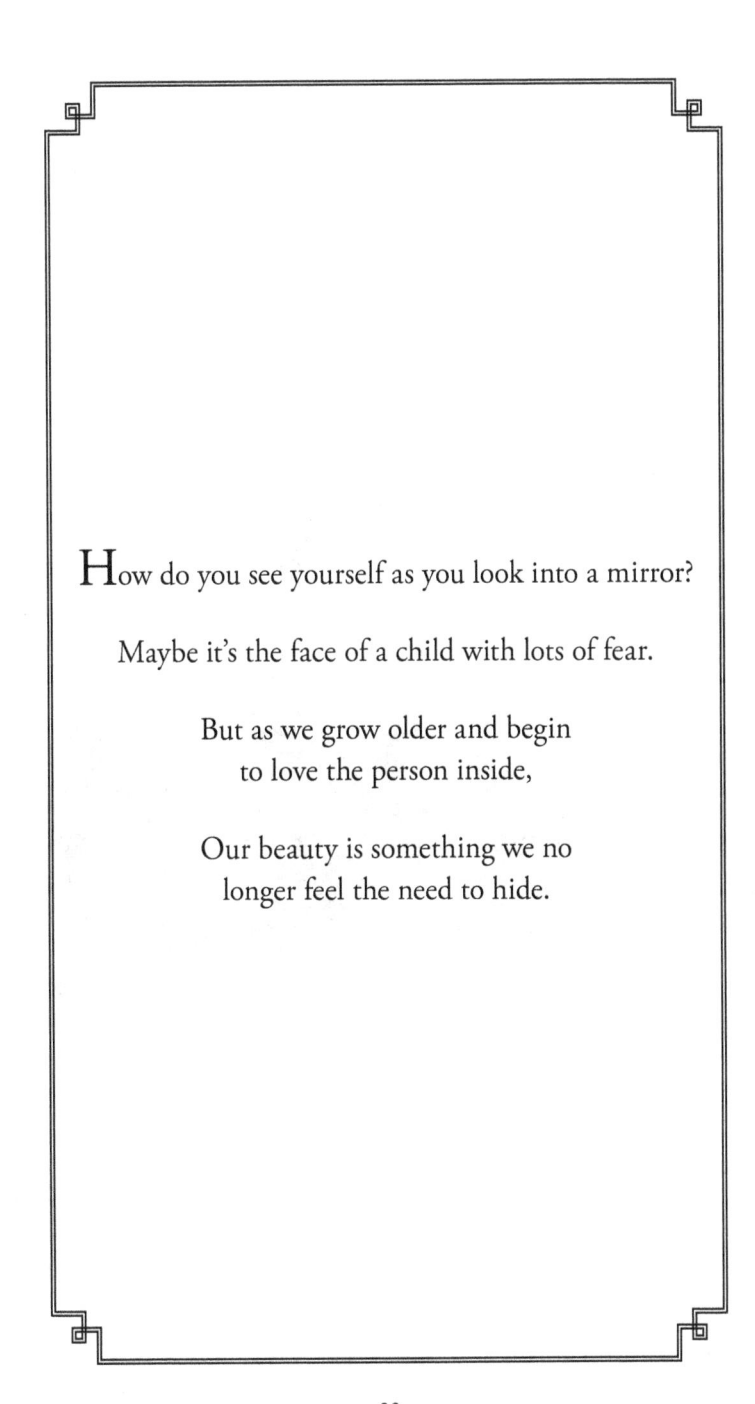

Maybe it's the face of a child with lots of fear.

But as we grow older and begin
to love the person inside,

Our beauty is something we no
longer feel the need to hide.

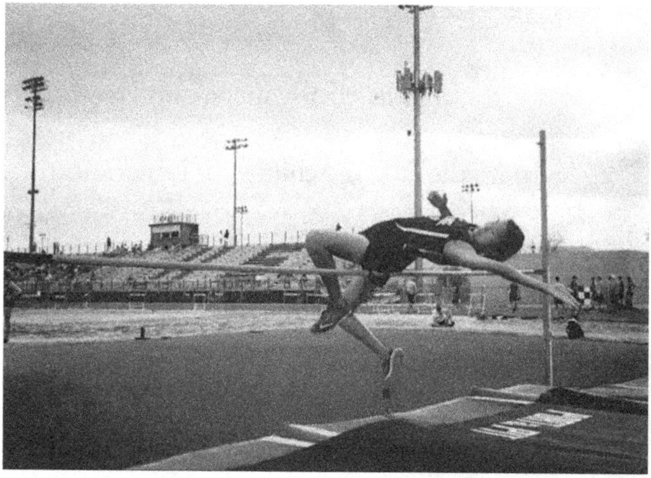

The bar is at its highest peak.
The confidence is now positive and not so weak.
So never believe that it can't be done—
Just one step forward, and you have won.

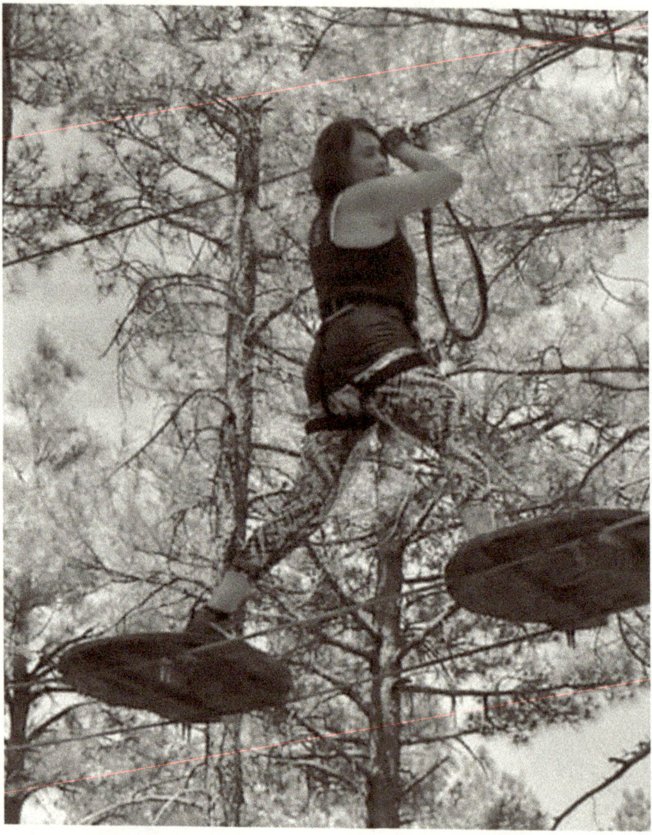

I know what you say is the right thing.
I know I have a strength that I can bring.
I know you say I am brave and need to fight.
I know what's ahead is a future so bright.
I know what I need, and that's not the shame.
I know what you say; I'm not to blame.
I know I can smile with no more pain.
I know when you say; I have so much to gain.
I know I have support and love.
I know that includes the man from up above.
I know I can trust and give my all.
I know you said not to quit and always stand tall.
I know I am capable of striving to the top.
I know you said it takes willpower to never stop.

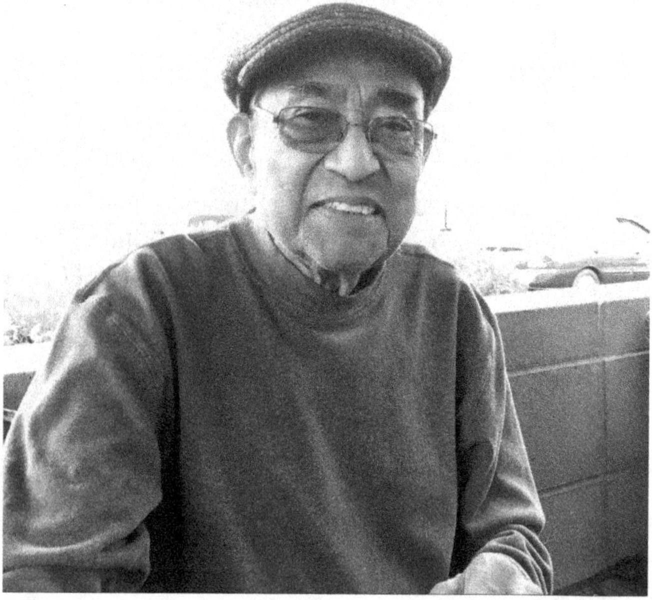

My dad is my hero with a heart of gold.

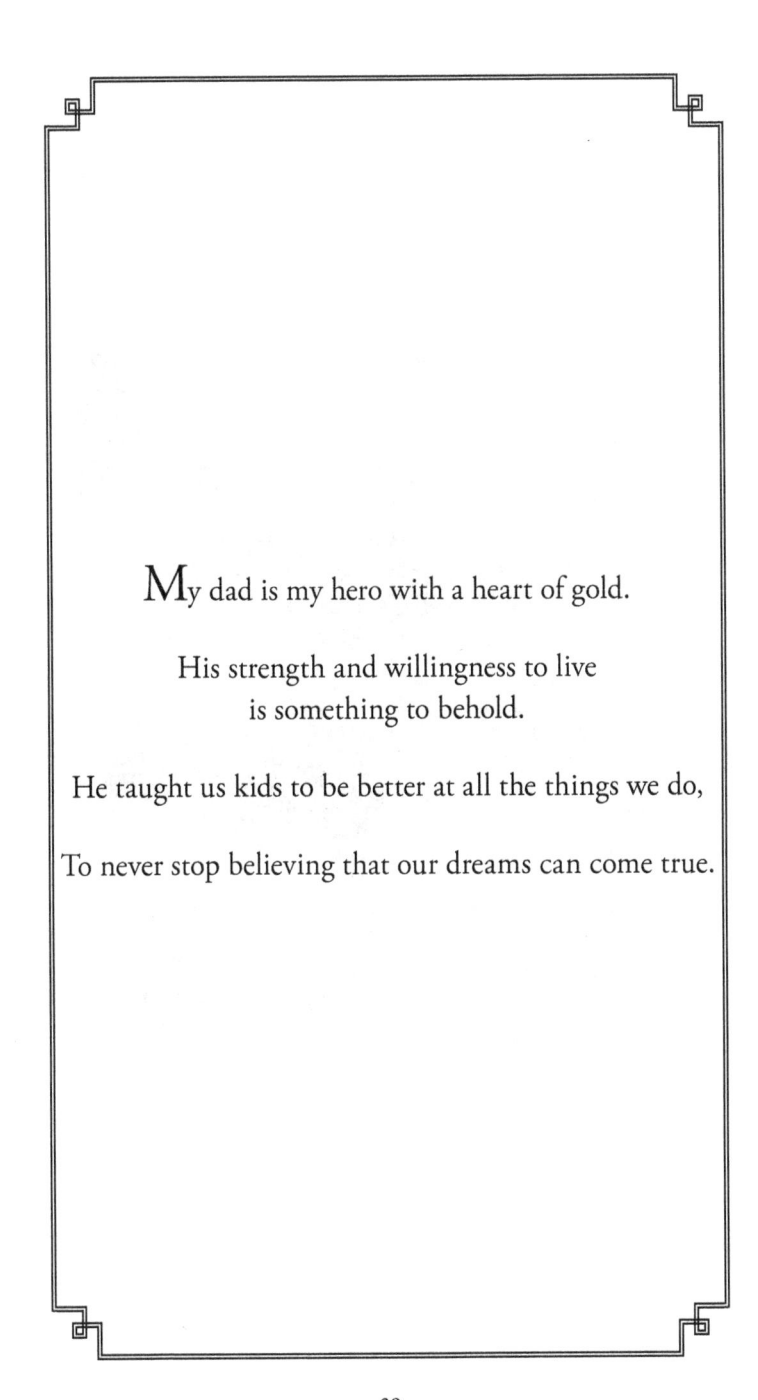

His strength and willingness to live
is something to behold.

He taught us kids to be better at all the things we do,

To never stop believing that our dreams can come true.

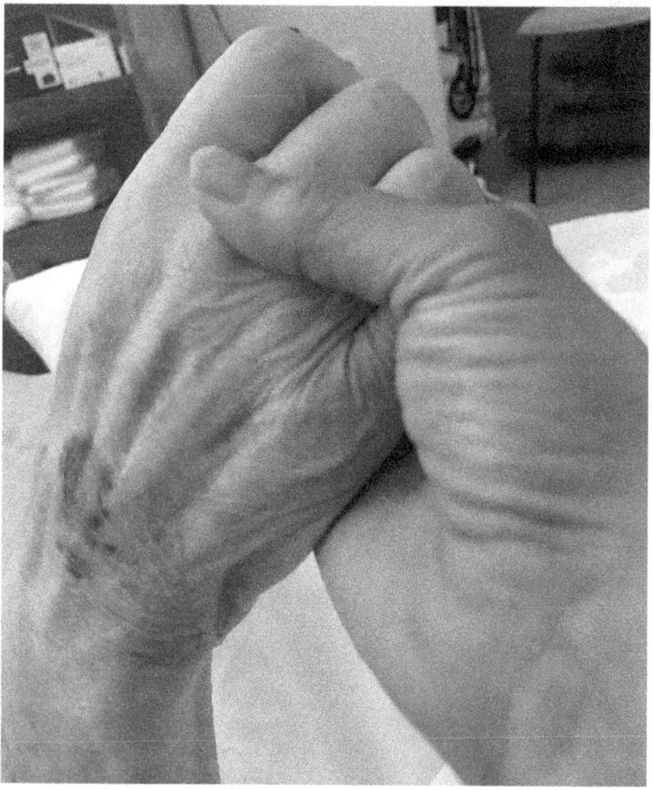

I held your hand the day you closed your eyes.

I talked to you and said my goodbyes.

You lay so peaceful, breathing slow.

I kissed your head and said, "It's okay to go."

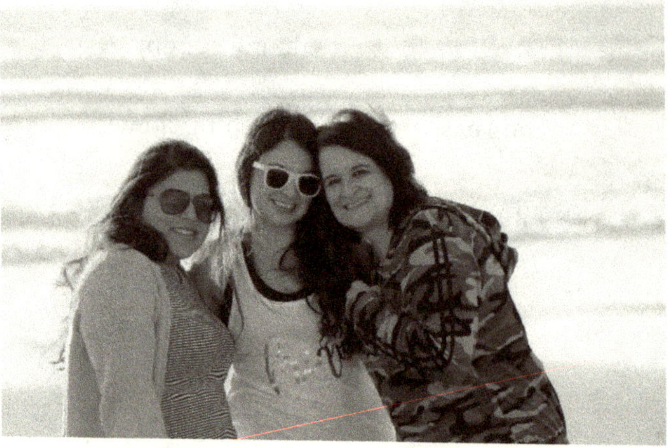

A mother and daughter's bond will never be forgotten.

We laugh, cry, and help each other when one has fallen.

Our hearts and love are things that are always opened.

We hold each other together until the end.

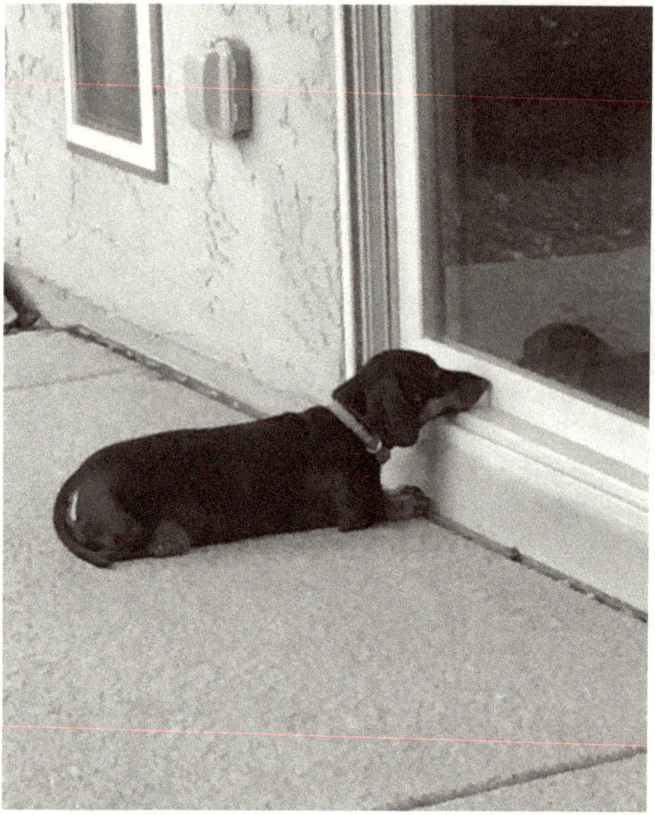

I'm grateful for the family I had.

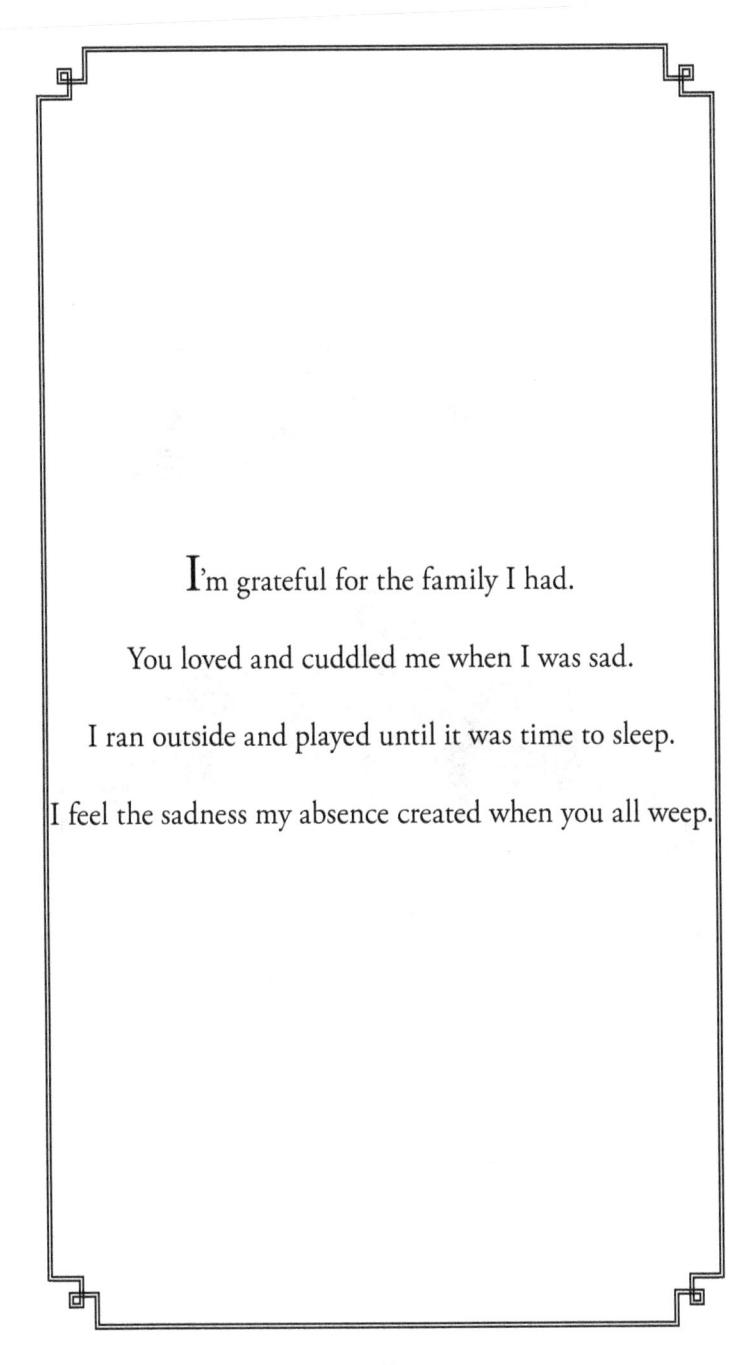

You loved and cuddled me when I was sad.

I ran outside and played until it was time to sleep.

I feel the sadness my absence created when you all weep.

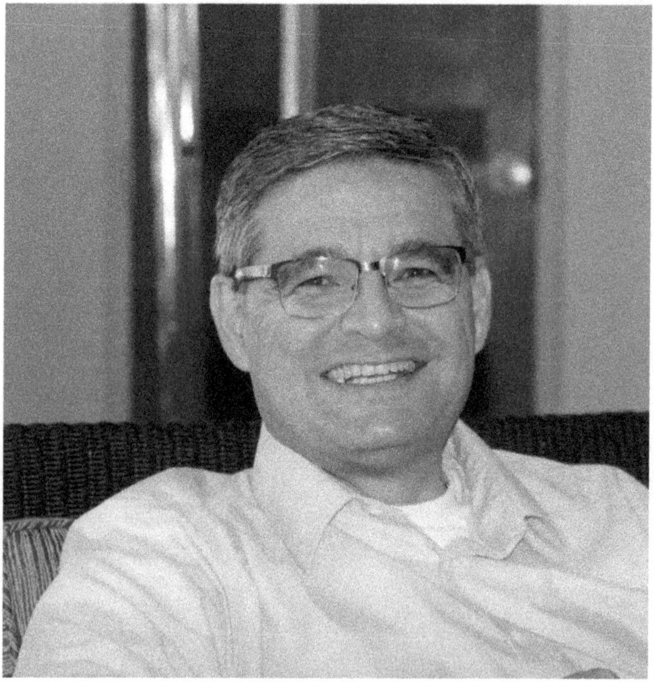

A brother is a gift that keeps us all together.

The heart he has is a great treasure.

A brother is someone you can
always depend on—

The comfort he gives when you
lose a special someone.

Printed in the USA
CPSIA information can be obtained
at www.ICGtesting.com
LVHW092143301223
767807LV00009B/438

9 781480 883741